Searchlight
BOOKS™

What
Is Digital
Citizenship?

Smart Online Communication

Protecting Your Digital Footprint

Mary Lindeen

Lerner Publications ◆ Minneapolis

D0859683

▶ For my great big, grown-up little brother, whose brain is a lot like the Internet: a storehouse of fascinating facts and random bits of information, including every embarrassing thing I've ever done

Lerner Publications Company
A division of Lerner Publishing Group, Inc.
241 First Avenue North
Minneapolis, MN 55401 USA

For reading levels and more information, look up this title at www.lernerbooks.com.

Library of Congress Cataloging-in-Publication Data

Lindeen, Mary, author.
   Smart online communication : protecting your digital footprint / Mary Lindeen.
      pages cm. — (Searchlight books. What is digital citizenship?)
   Audience: Ages 8–11.
   Audience: Grades 4 to 6.
   Includes bibliographical references and index.
   ISBN 978-1-4677-9487-9 (lb : alk. paper)
   ISBN 978-1-4677-9695-8 (pb : alk. paper)
   ISBN 978-1-4677-9696-5 (eb pdf)
   1. Internet and children—Safety measures—Juvenile literature. 2. Online social networks—Juvenile literature. 3. Social media—Safety measures—Juvenile literature. 4. Communication—Social aspects—Juvenile literature. I. Title.
   HQ784.I58L565 2016
   004.67'80835—dc23   2015021185

Manufactured in the United States of America
1 – VP – 12/31/15

Contents

Chapter 1
WHAT IS A DIGITAL FOOTPRINT?
. . . page 4

Chapter 2
WATCH YOUR STEP . . . page 14

Chapter 3
PROTECTING YOUR DIGITAL FOOTPRINT . . . page 22

Chapter 4
A FOOTPRINT IS FOREVER . . . page 30

Technology and the Digital Citizen • 37
Glossary • 38
Learn More about Online Communication • 39
Index • 40

WHAT IS A DIGITAL FOOTPRINT?

When you walk on the beach, you leave footprints in the sand. If you look over your shoulder as you walk, you can see the steps you've taken. And if someone else takes a walk on that same beach, they can see your trail of footprints too.

Your footprints show where you've walked. What does your digital footprint show?

You also leave a trail whenever you go online. Every search you make, website you visit, and photo you upload adds to this digital trail. The evidence of your online activity is called your digital footprint.

SEARCH ENGINES SUCH AS GOOGLE CAN TRACK YOUR ONLINE SEARCHES.

Tracking Software

Tracking software keeps a record of your online activity. Internet service providers, web browsers, and websites use tracking software. It tracks the sites you visit and the things you post online.

Most web browsers keep track of what you do online.

Some tracking software saves your log-in information.

A computer cookie is one kind of tracking software. This text file stores usernames, preference settings, and other information. Information stored on a cookie can allow a website to welcome you by name every time you go to that site. Cookies can also store your passwords. Then you don't have to enter them every time you log in to your accounts. Cookies aren't considered harmful. They don't carry viruses. They don't steal information from your computer.

Spyware is another kind of tracking software. Spyware downloads automatically when you download other things. For example, a free app you download to your tablet or phone might have spyware that comes with it. The spyware tracks your online activity. It sends that information to the owner of the app.

Apps that people download to their phones may have spyware.

Unlike cookies, spyware can be harmful. Spyware can steal passwords, e-mail addresses, and other information. It can track what you type. It can find information stored on your device. It can steal information from cookies. That information can then be used to steal your identity.

Did You Know?

Along with snooping through your information, spyware uses memory. Spyware is software. It takes up storage space on your digital devices. It constantly sends your information to the people who own the spyware. This can make your devices run slowly or even crash.

Not All Bad

Many different groups of people are interested in the information that makes up your digital footprint. Some have bad intentions. But others use the information for harmless or even helpful purposes.

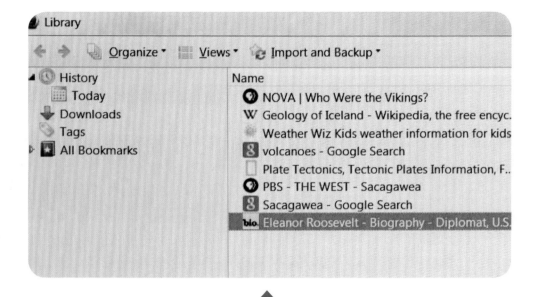

SOME PROGRAMS SAVE YOUR INFORMATION SO YOU DON'T HAVE TO ENTER A PASSWORD WHEN YOU LOG IN. THIS IS HELPFUL WHEN VISITING SITES YOU OFTEN GO TO, SUCH AS DATABASES THAT HELP YOU DO HOMEWORK.

Companies that sell things online want to know about their customers. This helps them serve customers better. For example, a shoe store might see that you are looking for sneakers online. It might use that information to show you ads for different sneakers. Having good customer service helps companies make more money.

Having good customer service, both online and off, is important to businesses.

Law enforcement officials use information they find online to catch criminals. Reporters look online for photos, quotes, and other information that can be used in news stories.

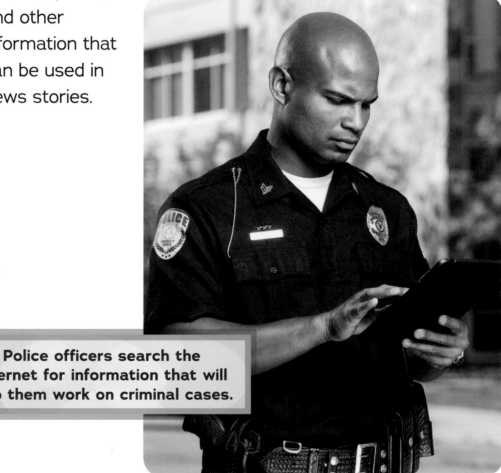

Police officers search the Internet for information that will help them work on criminal cases.

Your family and your school can use your digital footprint to help keep you safe. For example, your family can check the websites you visit. They can tell if strangers are talking to you online. Then they can block sites where strangers are trying to reach you. That way, you can browse safely.

Ask a parent or a guardian for permission before visiting a new website or downloading something from the Internet.

Chapter 2

WATCH YOUR STEP

While some online information gathering is used for good, it is still very important to be careful online. After all, the Internet can connect you with millions of people around the world. Some of these people are really great, but others are not.

Protecting your digital footprint can help you stay safe online. What is one way your digital footprint could be used against you?

Cyberbullying

Your digital footprint can be used against you if you are a victim of cyberbullying. Sending threatening e-mails to someone is cyberbullying. Using the Internet to make fun of someone is cyberbullying. Getting others to repeat rumors about someone online is cyberbullying. Victims of this kind of bullying may find that their e-mail addresses, contact lists, and online posts are used against them.

Cyberbullying is serious and harmful.

Hacking

Hacking is breaking into a software system. For example, hackers might break into a bank's software system to steal its information. This information includes bank customers' names, addresses, and account numbers.

HACKERS SOMETIMES USE PUBLIC COMPUTERS TO ACCESS OTHERS' PRIVATE INFORMATION.

With this information, hackers can transfer money to their own accounts. They can also sell that information to other hackers.

Hackers can steal from you if they have your information.

Did You Know?

Sometimes hacking can be useful. Hacking into a security system can point out its weak spots. Fixing those weaknesses then makes the security system stronger. Hacking can also be used to make something that is helpful or even beautiful. Making two software programs work together to create a work of art that neither program could have made on its own is an example of this kind of hacking.

Spam and Phishing

Advertisers can use your e-mail address to send unwanted ads to your inbox. These unwanted e-mails are called spam. Sometimes you can quickly tell that an e-mail message is spam. The message might include words like *Buy now!* or *Great deal!*

Other times, spam looks like an e-mail from a friend. The e-mail might ask you to visit a certain website. If you visit the site, it might send a virus to your computer. You can best protect yourself from spam by deleting it and never responding to it.

Be careful when you look at your e-mail. Spam can harm your computer.

Another kind of e-mail scam is called phishing. Phishing e-mails seem to be from real people or groups. The e-mails might ask for a password or the name of your school. Or they might send you to a website. The site will then ask you for personal information.

Hackers use phishing to get your personal information. They want to use it to steal your identity or your money. Always check with a trusted adult before you share any information online.

Talk to a trusted adult before you open any suspicious e-mails.

Your Own Worst Enemy

Other people are not the only ones who can use your digital footprint against you. Sometimes you can be your own worst enemy. People often forget that things they post online will be there forever. Other people can also download and share what you post. A photo you posted of you and your best friends wearing silly outfits and making goofy faces might get passed around to everyone at your school, whether you wanted it to or not.

Anything you post on the Internet may be seen by a lot of people.

Never post anything you don't want the whole world to see forever. Stop and think before you make a comment or put a picture online. A good rule to follow is to only post things that you would be comfortable putting on the door of your principal's office. If your post doesn't pass that test, do not put it online.

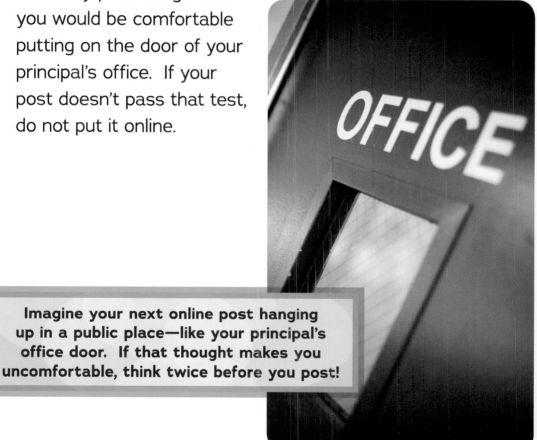

Imagine your next online post hanging up in a public place—like your principal's office door. If that thought makes you uncomfortable, think twice before you post!

Chapter 3

PROTECTING YOUR DIGITAL FOOTPRINT

Protecting your digital footprint means having a game plan. You can have fun online, but you have to be careful too. You can't guard your online identity completely. But a game plan can help you out.

Learning to be safe online is a must in our digital world. What is one important rule of online safety?

Game Plan

The most important part of any game plan for guarding your identity is to keep personal information private. Never give your name, age, home address, e-mail address, phone number, or other facts about yourself or your family to someone online that you don't know in person. You wouldn't share personal information with a stranger at the mall. Don't share that information with strangers online either.

Practice safety around strangers online, just as you would around strangers in a mall.

Most e-mail providers and social networking sites have privacy settings. They let you choose who sees what you post. Ask a trusted adult to help you use the privacy settings on your devices. Make sure you're using these settings correctly.

School technology specialists can help answer questions about online privacy settings.

TRUSTWORTHY WEBSITES OFTEN HAVE PRIVACY POLICIES.

Many websites also have privacy policies. A privacy policy is a set of rules the website follows to protect your privacy. Websites are allowed to collect and share some of the information they get from their customers. Their privacy policy lists the information they can collect. It also explains who they share that information with.

Your online accounts are usually protected by a password. Passwords are combinations of letters, numbers, and symbols that allow you to access your account. Your e-mail account is an example of an account that requires a password.

Your e-mail password helps protect your e-mail account from hackers.

It's a good idea to write down your passwords, but make sure you keep them in a secret place.

Usually you get to choose your own password. The best passwords are those that are hard for others to guess. A password that uses a mix of at least eight letters, numbers, and symbols is hard to guess.

Using different passwords for different accounts is another good idea. And keep your passwords private. Never share your passwords with anyone except a parent or guardian.

Another way to protect your digital identity is to be careful about the devices you use. Always log out of your accounts when you are done with them. This is especially important if you use a phone or computer at a library, school, or someone else's home. Whoever uses the device after you can get into your accounts if you don't log out. Make sure no one is looking over your shoulder when you log in to your accounts either. They can find out what your passwords are by watching the keys you type.

Always be careful when you use a public computer.

Use care when you are online too. Some websites have content that is not appropriate for kids your age. Close the web page and tell a trusted adult if you come to such a site.

Also tell an adult right away if someone online asks you to call or wants to meet you in person. Some people use the Internet to trick kids. These people pretend to be your friend to get you to trust them. That makes it easier for them to find you and hurt you. Always check with a trusted adult before you communicate with anyone online.

Tell a trusted adult if a stranger tries to talk to you online.

Chapter 4

A FOOTPRINT IS FOREVER

Footprints on a beach are easily washed away by waves. Your digital footprint is not so easily erased. The things you post online stay there forever. A comment you make on a website today could be there ten years from now.

What you post on the Internet may never be deleted. Why is it so important to be careful about what you post?

Mind Your Trail

Ten years from now, you might be applying for a job or to college. Employers and schools use the Internet to find out about people who send them applications. What will people see when they look you up online? Will they see things that make you proud? Or things that embarrass you?

WHEN YOU APPLY FOR A JOB, AN EMPLOYER MAY SEARCH FOR YOUR POSTS ONLINE.

Sometimes people make mistakes or change their minds. Something that seems funny to you now may embarrass you in the future. Or one of your friends might post a picture of you online without realizing that you wanted to keep it private. It can be even worse if someone puts false information about you online just to hurt you.

It can be fun to post silly pictures of you and your friends. But be careful not to post things that might embarrass you or someone else.

Content shared on the Internet can spread extremely quickly.

You can sometimes remove things that have been posted online. You can delete some of the things you post yourself. Someone else who posts something about you might not be willing to delete it. Sometimes you don't even know who posted information about you. And sometimes, the information posted gets shared with so many people that it's not possible to find and delete every copy of it. It stays on the Internet for everyone to see forever.

One of the best ways to protect yourself online is to always be your best self when you're on the Internet. Don't make mean comments. Don't use bad language. Don't say anything online that you wouldn't say to your family. Only visit websites that are appropriate for kids your age. That way, you're less likely to see something that might scare you or make you feel uncomfortable. Ask an adult to help you find sites that are good for you to visit.

As long as you're smart about what you put online, the Internet can be a lot of fun!

Think about your skills. Think about the things you do well. Think about the person you are and the person you want to become. Make sure the comments and pictures you post are things you can be proud of. Let your digital image be the best image of your true self.

YOU WORK HARD TO BE RESPONSIBLE AT SCHOOL. MAKE SURE TO BE RESPONSIBLE WITH YOUR ONLINE REPUTATION TOO!

Be a Good Digital Citizen

Your digital footprint shows others who you are and where you have been online. It tells people what you do, how you think, and what you are interested in. It is important to learn how to protect both your privacy and your reputation on the Internet. Anyone old enough to be online is also old enough to learn how to stay safe. So be a good digital citizen, and take smart steps to protect yourself today!

Your digital footprint says a lot about you. Be careful to protect it.

Technology and the Digital Citizen

Most people use passwords to protect their information online. But in the future, most of us might use our own thumbprints! Instead of typing a password to log in to a smartphone or a tablet, we might simply place our thumbs against the screen. Then a scanner in the device will "read" our thumbprint. If the scanner recognizes the thumbprint, the device will unlock.

It is much harder to steal someone's thumbprint than it is to steal someone's password. Thumbprints are unique to us, which makes them great for security. And new security innovations are cropping up every day. Someday, we might give up passwords altogether and instead rely on the sound of our voices or the shapes of our faces—in addition to our thumbprints—to help protect our information.

Glossary

app: a software program that is usually used on a smartphone or a tablet computer. *App* is short for *application*.

cookie: a usually harmless type of tracking software that stores screen names, preference settings, and other information

cyberbullying: when someone uses cell phones, computers, and other forms of technology to tease, frighten, or threaten someone else

digital footprint: the evidence of your online activity

hacking: breaking into a software system

phishing: sending e-mails that ask for information such as passwords or the name of your school, or that send you to a website that asks for personal information. Hackers often use phishing to steal people's money or identities.

software: computer programs that control the way electronic equipment works

spam: unwanted e-mail advertisements

spyware: a potentially harmful type of tracking software that can steal passwords, e-mail addresses, and other information and send it to another person

virus: hidden instructions within a computer program designed to destroy a computer system or damage data

LERNER

SOURCE

Expand learning beyond the printed book. Download free, complementary educational resources for this book from our website, www.lerneresource.com.

Learn More about Online Communication

Books

Lindeen, Mary. *Digital Safety Smarts: Preventing Cyberbullying*. Minneapolis: Lerner Publications, 2016. Read this title to get up-to-date information about the forms cyberbullying can take and how you can help prevent it.

Minton, Eric. *Passwords and Security*. New York: PowerKids, 2014. This book reminds readers that they may not have control over who sees their online information and suggests steps they can take to protect themselves online.

Schwartz, Heather E. *Safe Social Networking*. Mankato, MN: Capstone, 2013. Find out what to do in different online situations, such as if a stranger tries to contact you.

Websites

KidsHealth
http://kidshealth.org/kid/watch/house/internet_safety.html
Learn more about how to protect yourself online.

NetSmartzKids: Adventure Games
http://www.netsmartzkids.org/AdventureGames
Visit this site to play a game about Internet safety.

Safekids: Kids' Rules for Online Safety
http://www.safekids.com/kids-rules-for-online-safety
Check out this site to find helpful rules for safe Internet use.

Index

apps, 8

cookies, 7, 9
cyberbullying, 15

digital footprint, 5, 10, 13, 15, 20, 22, 30, 36

hacking, 16–17

passwords, 7, 9, 26–28, 37
phishing, 18–19
privacy policies, 25
privacy settings, 24

spam, 18
spyware, 8–9

Photo Acknowledgments

The images in this book are used with the permission of: © Anzhely.K/Shutterstock.com, p. 4; © Denys Prykhodov/Shutterstock.com, p. 5; © dolphfyn/Alamy, p. 6; © iStockphoto.com/mishooo, p. 7; © Helen Sessions/Alamy, p. 8; © Todd Strand/Independent Picture Service, pp. 10, 25; © Tom Merton/OJO Images/Getty Images, p. 11; © Jacom Stephens/Getty Images, p. 12; © Martin Barraud/Caiaimage/Getty Images, p. 13; © JGI/Jamie Grill/Blend Images/Getty Images, p. 14; © Peter Dazeley/Getty Images, pp. 15, 34; © iStockphoto.com/baona, p. 16; © Westend61/Getty Images, p. 17; © Feng Yu/Alamy, p. 18; © Hero Images/Getty Images, pp. 19, 33, 36; © damircudic /Vetta/Getty Images, p. 20; © iStockphoto.com/slobo, p. 21; © iStockphoto.com/Christopher Futcher, p. 22; © Urbanmyth/Alamy, p. 23; © Thomas Barwick/Getty Images, p. 24; © Epoxydude /fStop/Getty Images, p. 26; © iStockphoto.com/4774344sean, p. 27; © Michael Goldman/Getty Images, p. 28; © iStockphoto.com/mamahoohooba, p. 29; © Marc Romanelli/Blend Images /Getty Images, p. 30; © Andrew Paterson/Alamy, p. 31; © damircudic/Vetta/Getty Images, p. 32; © Elisabeth Schmitt/Moment/Getty Images, p. 35.

Front cover: © iStockphoto.com/Mark Bowden.

Main body text set in Adrianna Regular 14/20.
Typeface provided by Chank.